Leonard,
I hope you can glean
Something from these

Gleanings

John Liddy
Madrid
2010

Gleanings

JOHN LIDDY

POETRY

A REVIVAL POETRY BOOK

Revival Press
Limerick - Ireland

First published by
Revival Press,
Limerick, Ireland

www.revivalpress.com

In association with
The Limerick Writers' Centre

http://limerickwriterscentre.wordpress.com

www.facebook.com/limerickwriterscentre

Book design: Kelly Richards Printing
Cover Artwork: Natalie Stone
Cover Design: Aisling Burke

Project editor: Dominic Taylor

ISBN 978-0-9554722-8-2

A CIP catalogue record for this book is available from The British Library

We acknowledge the support of
www.limerick.com & The Limerick Writers' Centre

Community Driven
Limerick.com

Gleanings

for

José Luis and Mila

CONTENTS

Gleanings:

...from the margins:

Introduction

The birthplace may be Cork but the soul of this poet is a Limerick soul,
Limerick bred, coddled and exiled. John Liddy in his exile, his performances
and his editorial work, maintains an honoured and distinctive Limerick
tradition of cosmopolitan homeliness and distant yearning. He is the
inheritor of that tendency to be elsewhere; to be in Rome like Desmond
O'Grady or in New York like Frank McCourt. Each note he sings in these
poems, each interjection he offers, is saturated with a native centredness,
with a possessive sense of exile:

> *'For when we would look*
> *out the high window*
> *to allow thought roam,*
> *contemplate a tea-towel*
> *waving both of us home.'*

So that home, here, is a domestic place with two geographies: the
literary and social landscape of Limerick and the familiar, intimate
immediacy of an apartment in Madrid. Liddy has spent the greater part
of his adulthood in Hernandez's and Lorca's land, Spain, and an
authentic, lived-in, family-centred Spain emerges from these pages. His
understanding of this cultural disconnection, this binary European
existence of many Irish intellectuals, is sophisticated and cleverly
distilled in many of the poems. In 'Sorolla's Garden' he is deeply aware
of an exile's accentuated sense of being, so much so that he begins to use
the personality of the disconnected as a teaching weapon:

> *'I was part of the décor in this haven,*
> *Made of it a vital ingredient*
> *To teach my students all the better.'*

But it is Spain, as home and authority, that distinguishes the distinctive
personality of Liddy in poems – Spain with its smells and mountains,
its cafes and vibrant poetries. In Spain he found an adulthood after the
prolonged adolescence of Ireland. Madrid has taken to him like a portly
father-in-law, welcoming and familial Madrid; a Madrid that welcomed
so many of the best Irish, from the priestly scholars who were part
of the exiled courts of the Ulster Earls to the young diplomat poet
Máire Mhac an tSaoí. What Spain means is captured perfectly in his
masterful poem 'A Tree House In Jaen:'

> *'I like to imagine it intact,*
> *defiant after all those years*

> despite time and what winter
> does to everything in its path.
> A den for children in summer,
> high above the din of fields
> ablaze in a furnace of crickets,
> a shade in the afternoon sun
> descending on a day's adventure,
> the cold black drone of the Sierra
> de Segura in their dreams.'

Here, in poems like 'Francis Bacon in Madrid' and 'Sorolla's Garden' Spain is captured, also, for his homebound readers. But much of the poetry here looks back to the windswept island, an island overwhelmed by history, memory and volcanic ash. The past is redeemed by redemptive characters, street personalities, musicians, fathers, mothers and poets. His poem on Fonsie Renihan, Limerick newspaper-vendor and opera buff, is a classic of provincial memory. There is a Fonsie in every small provincial city in Europe, but this is pure Limerick, humility and grandeur combined: Fonsie and Beniamino Gigli. When thanked for the complimentary ticket and complimented by the paper-seller for his rendering of Ponchielli's 'La Gioconda' Gigli replies with a mysterious grace:

> "No, no" Gigli protested,
> "Thank you most sincerely
> for allowing me to see."
> Years later Fonsie talked
> about postcards from Beni.
> But what did he mean by
> allowing him to see?
> I often asked and never
> received an answer.
> Perhaps it was as Montaigne
> said: because it was him;
> because it was me.'

The encounter is pure Limerick, but the incident captured and mediated by Liddy is both provincial and Spanish: what both men have is what Lorca recognised, 'soul', 'Duende' a respect for life, for the life force that flows between men and women, a recognition of what is holy. This force of perception, the very soul of what's life-giving, the very essence of the poetic impulse, is what John Liddy has in spades, in bouquets, in essences of cigarillo smoke and campfires. This book is full of such snapshots, pin-ups of guardian angels, mementos of family, of Spain and Ireland. In terms of the force of memory, Ireland does win out here. In 'Decent Burials,' dedicated to Ian Gibson, Liddy joins Spain and Ireland, not the inventors of civil wars, but pure artists when it came to civil war capacity for mindless cruelty and residual hatred: 'the page turns like a sod to let the light in' is a powerful simile of poetry's redemptive, healing force. In poems like 'The Bible Garden in Glenstal', 'Tully Lane, Fenagh, County Leitrim' or 'Cromwell's Arch' Liddy recovers the old sod fully, with the meditative paintwork of story-telling, a sense of place and a sense of history reminiscent of the work of Montague or Richard Murphy. ' I salute them all and many more of their kind' as he writes.

But the poem that acts as a summary and a declaration of loyalties here, a wonderful poem in the tradition of Montague's 'Like Dolmens Round My Childhood' or Heaney's ''Squarings' is the wide-ranging, multi-layered elegy 'From Our Sad Heights.' Here, Liddy assembles the voices of the august dead, of family and fellow poets, of those Irish like his cousin James who died abroad as well as those dead in Cork like the poet Gregory O'Donoghue. It is the complete soul again, the singer's slow and deeply mediated remembrance. In this mosaic of exile that tells us so much of the power of family and friendship, Liddy creates a compelling narrative. Where, as poets, do we get authority? Is it from suffering, imprisonment, exile, insightful political genius? Liddy knows that it is none and all of these things, but the glue that holds it all together is the blood of being human. 'From Our Sad Heights' brings the Liddy narrative of exile right up to date, to President Obama's victory rally in Chicago reaching Milwaukee. The poet, like the cousin in America, recognised a voice that was saturated with life, with community service, and with a vision that might redeem an entire people. Liddy, like the wonderful big-hearted souls of Limerick, the Merrimans, the McCourts, the O'Gradys, knows that a poem could save the whole world. Here, then, and in the pages that follow, are the words that save us:

> 'Perhaps my cousin's eyes shone with the news
> Before they closed – a donation to Obama's
> Campaign fund was money well disposed.
> Maybe he saw words from the victory speech
> Float round his bed like butterflies and petals
> Before heavenly peace on earth was made.
> His final rally a gathering in the mind of all
> That he loved in life, the poetry of people....'

Thomas McCarthy

A TEA TOWEL

for Milagros

After each visit we looked back
from the road across the field
to delight in you waving us home
with a tea towel I wished
we could have waved for you.

But not one for travel,
you held your own destination
in the privacy of your mind,
lighting up at its mention
especially at Christmas time

Surrounded by your brood,
whose curiosity for stories
about their gaditana origins
beside the Ocean,
knew no end.

Never a cross word
between us, we are more
than friends, and those casual
chats in the Robledo kitchen
were exactly the right ingredients

For when we would look
out the high window
to allow thought roam,
contemplate a tea-towel
waving both of us home.

PAÑO DE COCINA

para Milagros

Después de cada visita miramos hacia atrás
del camino a través del campo
para deleitarnos con tu paño de cocina
agitado desde tu casa, lamentando
no poder agitarlo para ti.

Viajar no siendo lo suyo, sostienes tu propio destino
en la intimidad de tu mente, que se enciende
al mencionarlo sobre todo en Navidades
rodeada de tu familia, cuya curiosidad
por historias sobre sus orígenes gaditanos

Al lado del océano no tiene fin.
Sin una palabra malsonante entre nosotros,
somos más que amigos; aquellas charlas
ocasionales en la cocina de Robledo
fueron exactamente los ingredientes

Correctos para que cuando miremos
a través de la alta ventana nos permita
que un pensamiento vuela,
contemplar un paño de cocina
agitándonos de vuelta a casa.

A TREE HOUSE IN JAEN

for Rubin

I like to imagine it intact,
defiant after all those years
despite time and what winter
does to everything in its path.

A den for children in summer,
high above the din of fields
ablaze in a furnace of crickets,
a shade in the afternoon sun
descending on a day's adventure,
the cold black drone of the Sierra
de Segura in their dreams.

Perhaps it shelters washed-up
immigrants or wounded hawks,
incommunicado hill walkers, a shrine
for those who believe it to be holy,
where miracles happen on days
when the *Romaría* lays out its picnic,
contemplates the apparition.

I like to think the knots as tight
as moored boats in a storm,
the log-walls and floor snug
in the crotch of the old holm-oak,
knifed with initials proclaiming
the existence of a hedge school

That once echoed with laughter
and the silence of leaves on faces
grown to be their own trees
in the thick of cities
where everything can seem
splintered and disposable.

AMNESIA

Round up the accordion players of Europe
The voice ordains, along with the carers
Of the elderly and the feeble, those Florence
Nightingales of the better neighbourhoods,
Home helpers, cheap labourers, car park
Attendants and all those non-nationals.

Send them packing, the voice clamours,
Bomb them by the boatful before landing.
To hell with inter-state accords and treaties,
They rob us of our jobs and our women,
A place in the queue for social services,
Boarding-cards, elbow-room at the bar.

But who will sooth the voice should it
Croak to slake its thirst on foreign streets,
Beg for pittance with a parched throat
Without a squeak to keep it company?
For this righteous voice is loud with pious
Platitudes and short on historical memory.

BLUE BEAUTY
for Doc and Astronaut Dan Tani

While he was orbiting Earth Dan's mother died
Overtaking his old school bus at a level crossing.
He could have attended the funeral via satellite
Connection but opted instead for a space walk.

What he saw was truly of this world.
The Oceans defying gravity, great river gods
Born as mountain trickles, a sandstorm advancing
On the Canaries and the Antarctic diminishing.

But what really caught his eye was the thin line
Between abundance and scarcity, night and day,
The twilight zone. It was then he saw the need
For cohabitating a volatile beauty, the meaning

Of being alone yet sharing the one cell.
By way of confirmation he felt his mother go by
On her ascent from heaven, bound for a distant
Star on this his forty-seventh birthday.

The umbilical link to the craft not lost on him
In the darkness of his own crossing.

CROMWELL'S ARCH

Under the crenellated top of Water Gate's
Pointed archway, I was able to imagine
A stern man with a self-satisfied expression
For a job well done, trotting out of Youghal
Towards a ship at the ready to take him
Away to England, never to return.

Perhaps I saw in the sudden gush of water
From behind a closed door, (spilling out
Onto the laneway, splashing my shoes)
Blood flowing in the gully and heard
His horse's hooves on the cobbles,
Sparking An Eochaill ablaze.

I could feel a stultified growth in the old
Stones of the Base Town, divine how such
A driven man made a country tremble,
Curse its people to hell or to Connaught.
But there have been others since then
With different weapons, as brutal.

From today's perspective men like him
Still sack villages, slit throats and plunder.
They too will have gateways or arches
Named after them, localized to renew
The memory of future generations
As they freely pass through.

DECENT BURIALS

for Ian Gibson

1. Ireland

Some locals believe a Black and Tan soldier
May be buried in the centre of Gort bog,
Lixnaw, outside Tralee, under bramble and fern.

He was the result of an IRA execution during the War
Of Independence – reprisals abounded on both sides –
Terrible things were done, there were no angels.

They would like to see him returned to his people
In England, exhumed and given a decent burial
No matter what the wrong or the right of the thing

Because old wounds fester beneath the surface
And time cannot assuage the memory until the page
Turns like a sod to allow light in, a fresh beginning.

2. Spain

The body-politic cannot agree on unearthing Civil War
Atrocity, brush away the dust of secrecy, allow living
Relatives some semblance of relief for lost dignity.

One such pit in a private field beside the Burgos motorway
Contained the bones of four brothers (and four others)
Who were taken out on August 14, 1936 –

Their mother went blind from the sadness of her loss.
In time, no doubt, there will be other places uncovered
To reveal the horror for both sides to find consensus

And decent burial not seen as reprisal for repression
but a release from the suffocating weeds of memory,
Lorca's wish for definitive reconciliation.

EL REPOSO DE BAGHDAD

In the centre of the patio
a fountain vaporises
the desert heat of the street.

Abundant flora perfume
and shade the cool-tiled interior
which hums of harmony

As we take tea on enormous
cushions surrounded
by walls of florid script.

Such tranquillity is at odds
with news from the invaded city,
death and destruction

The source of my pity
here in calm Cordoba
of Al Andalus, Christian, Jew.

A palpable peace
in this resting place.

EYEWITNESS

for six year old Claudia O'Donnell

I was feeding straw to the cows
when a man led a woman on a donkey
into the stable and laid her down
where it was soft and warm.

After a while I heard life's first cry
and the music of doves in the rafters.
The whole place lit up like a palace
and people came from afar

To kneel beside the baby's cot.
One day three Kings arrived with gifts
and I must say I felt very proud
to be a stable boy in Bethlehem.

Years later I heard that the baby
grew to be a great leader
and performed many miracles
that included walking on water.

I also heard he was crucified
and I often thought of that night
when he was born, the dove songs
and the strange light that shone.

FONSIE AND BENI

i.m Fonsie Renihan

When Beniamino Gigli
alighted from Limerick station,
he met Alphonsus Renihan
outside The Railway Hotel.
"Welcome" he said, "you
brought the house down
last night in Dublin and met
your friend, Madam Sheridan –
Maggie from Mayo."

Gigli, surprised to hear
this news vendor's rapport,
enquired if he were coming
to the concert that evening.
"I would if I had a ticket",
replied Fonsie, "we all want
to hear Caruso's successor"
and with that Gigli insisted
he accept a complimentary.

The next morning he came
for the papers and Fonsie
mentioned that his rendering
of Ponchielli's La Gioconda
was superb and thanked him
for the invitation.
"No, no" Gigli protested,
"Thank you most sincerely
for allowing me to see."

Years later Fonsie talked
about postcards from Beni.
But what did he mean by
allowing him to see?
I often asked and never
received an answer.
Perhaps it was as Montaigne
said: *because it was him;*
because it was me.

FRANCIS BACON IN MADRID

Today I thought of you, Francis Bacon,
When Velazquez eyed me from his pedestal,
Caught my sorrow with a brush stroke
As though he knew I had heard the cries
Of burning bodies in a plane crash,
'The sucking sound of human flesh
Torn from living bone'.

It was a raw sensation and I felt boxed in
Like a Beckettian character in a bin,
Unable to comfort the victim,
Console the living with God's will.
But in the midst of such pain
You came to mind and your last days
In Madrid with friends, dining on oysters

And champagne, before finding peace
In the Ruber Clinic with a view of a crucifix
Over your bed and your own crucifixion
Attended by two adorable nuns.
How strange for one who saw through
Pomp and benign authority, caught
The hallucination in Pope Innocent X,

To end your days like this. You, who
Would have surpassed the condolences
With a painting of such galvanic effect
That the paint would sing in exaltation,
Move mind into light beyond banality.
A more fitting memorial to despair
And eventual recovery.

FROM A CABIN WINDOW IN LUND, BC
for David Wise

First thing each morning I would scan the line
Of beach for the unusual, hear snow falling
From sun-drenched treetops and ponder the Pacific
Wave breasting the shore beside Highway 101
That stretched as far as Chile.

Since the words I worked on proved obstinate,
Reluctant to reveal their true selves,
I was glad for the stroll to the village founded
By two Swedish brothers who, in 1889,
Named this place after their home town.

On one trip up the coast in David's trawler
I met draft dodgers, fishermen and loggers
Who turned wood into works of domestic art.
Alaska beckoned but home was calling him
To meet his love back from India.

She had been searching for tranquility,
Peace of mind and a way to accept uncertainty,
The imperfections of this world. I remember
Thinking I had glimpsed the answer here
From the window, the source of her search.

When I looked out for the last time
I saw a man dashing to the saffron-blazing shore.
I shied from their embrace to pack and contemplate
For more than thirty years that framed moment
When three people found lucidity in the grove.

FROM OUR SAD HEIGHTS

And you, my father, there on the sad height,
Curse, bless me now with your fierce tears, I pray.

Dylan Thomas

1.
The deaths of close ones undo me.
Rodriquez, Hierro, Gonzalez -
Each has gored my core with their passing.

And there will be others under this Spanish sky
To pike me with their farewells,
As those Irish have done –

Hartnett, O'Donoghue, Liddy –
Left me bereft to carry on,
Nourishing with their words my fragile song.

2.
Perhaps my cousin's eyes shone with the news
Before they closed – a donation to Obama's
Campaign fund was money well disposed.

Maybe he saw words from the victory speech
Float round his bed like butterflies and petals
Before heavenly peace on earth was made.

His final rally a gathering in the mind of all
That he loved in life, the poetry of people
And place on both sides of the Atlantic.

Everything reminding James of the journey
With Liam for company and Jim by his side,
Chicago's Grant Park cheering him in Milwaukee.

3.
Pamela was unusually quiet as we lingered
Outside the school gates she had entered
And left for thirty years, as I still do.

Pausing to see me through
I saw her mouth form a goodbye,
A pretence of dust from the street in her eye.

After a last lunch with Mariana
She was gone, left us with the eulogy
And the song. Mo chara, comrade, amiga.

4.
I heard Nuala say on the radio how she would miss
Her one-room oasis in New York, the smell of coffee
In Parisian bars, the courtesy of Madrid's Hotel Ritz.

She joked there was not much wrong with her
Except that she was dying, even quoting a poem
In Irish about Christ – strong-willed, agnostic lover

And adding with a killer punch what a waste creation
Is because she would take so much with her nobody
Knows about, leave all she knows behind.

5.
Uncle Rory in his Sunday best shook my hand
While saying farewell. He was gone within the time
It takes the train to get from Limerick to Dublin.

He must have readied himself immediately after
We had left, lain there thinking, his duty done
Like Felix Randal – fearless, unflinching, stoical.

6.

Father in his wisdom staked his claim on his spot
With a cross and two years later Marcus was laid to rest.
Mother, who loved life, refused to visit the grave.

Too sad for flowers, she said, yet followed without complaint.
While waiting for final arrangements I was asked by a nun
To talk with a man in the next room, he was terminally

Afraid, refused to accept his condition. I mentioned
Maureen's face and how it glowed as she went,
So he nodded with softening eyes at what had been spent.

7.

I salute them all and many more of their kind.
Who, from their sad heights, knew when to embrace
The toll of unique time, believed something achieved

Within the allotted space. Noble torch-bearers
Passing on the flame. Each one a veritable act of dignity,
Lessons for the living embroiled in life's comedy.

LIFE AND DEATH IN THE KITCHEN

I had been idling at the table all morning,
watching mother greasing the baking tin,
smoothing out the pastry with a wet fork.

Over several cups of tea we talked
about life as though it were a subject
removed from us. Stories unfolded

And kind words were offered in defence
of wronged neighbours. The warmth
and smell of blackberry kept us

At it until father suddenly appeared,
carrying something wrapped in sackcloth.
He had been away all morning 'on business'

And went out the back for a thin brush,
a pot of white paint. The tart was placed
by the window to cool and as we lifted

The first slice to our mouths he laid
an iron cross before us with his name
and date of birth. 'This will mark my spot

In Donoughmore' he joked, and with that
mother poured the tea and cut another slice
in silence as the juice and the paint mingled.

NIGHT CLASS IN GREEK TRAGEDY

Whenever Mammon falls from grace,
Those who ignored the warnings
Of the true Gods can fill the emptiness
By discovering how Zephyr,
Out of much misery and foul deed
Blew Aphros ashore,
How beautiful Aphrodite was born.

Successful applicants are required
To undertake some practical work
By squatting with the poor in Sodom's
Moneyed doorways and pondering
How plenty was squandered for more.

In this way, survivors learn why Cronos
Gobbled his children, set a precedent
For greed that has never waned.
Because this is how it all began –
Gaea created *adamant* from Chaos,
A yawning abyss on Earth's solid platform.
Students are taught to keep Eros close.

THE ECHO OF THE HOWL

In the Occupied Territories
there are Jewish only roads.
People wait at checkpoints
to have their arms stamped.

I am reminded of a man
who rolled up his sleeve
to show me his number.
He was once a nameless

Boy in rags who walked
out of a liberated camp
along a dirt path towards
a promised land.

In the West Bank children
are shot going to school
or blown to smithereens
by suicide bombers.

Essentials are restricted,
genocide a real possibility,
a repeat performance
to appease the memory

Of the Shoah, liquidation
by expert dice throwers
with all the numbers
up their sleeves.

Perhaps victims seek
to be cleansed of pain
borne with God's blessing
to do their own killing,

Suppress the howl's echo
with distortions of lessons
on what was done to them.
As for the man who showed

Me his arm, maybe he too
has rolled up other sleeves,
branded much flesh
of the herd.

RICHARD PIGOTT'S FORGERY

The day before Pigott supposedly shot himself
In a Madrid hotel, an interpreter showed him around.
On tour he may have taken notes about places he saw
And I wonder was the word *hesitancy* on his mind?

Perhaps he sensed his own betrayal on the street
Of the Irish, a wasted life in the splendor of the Plaza
Mayor or a feeling of being followed in Sol
From where all roads begin and end.

A letter was found on his body, ready for mailing.
He said he would remedy all that was false,
Expressed remorse for those he had perjured
And also asked for money promised.

In his room there was a license issued in Dublin
To carry a revolver, along with uncashed cheques –
No proof of identity – scribblings in a notebook
Penned by this poor forger who was *unhesitent*

In his unionism but a piggoted nationalist – as vilified
In Joyce's Wake by Shem – who had tried
To incriminate Parnell in the Phoenix Park murders.
Orders were given for a decent burial.

SHINNORS AS SCARECROW
for Catherine

Under a plastic canopy
like an invention to trap the rain,
I saw images sway on metal hooks,
riverwind scatter loose tobacco
like seed across a flooded field
to float in the cloud's shadow.

There where you scarecrowed
on the fringe of market morning,
I placed deposits on what caught my eye:
fish heads puzzled about separation,
night lights on train tracks
beguiling a leaky station.

Later in our local I praised
the guardians of pea and wheat field,
while you listened in silence
to visions of empty sockets,
devised ways of seeing:

A swallow's view of a lighthouse,
Looping kites beyond horizons,
A sense of place on the estuary,
The river never far from your gaze,
A sense of a woman's presence.

SOROLLA'S GARDEN

Sapped by the city's manic haste
I found my retreat from the noise
And the heat in a painter's
Garden where I could imagine
Longed-for-places, thick-ferned
And mossed like fertile groves,
The fountain in the centre a cool
Spray fanning me with sea breeze.

Sometimes I was the Moro
Who sold oranges nobody bought
Or a Valentian guitarist wooing
A woman with love songs.
I could step into any canvass –
Be a fisherman's son with a toy boat
Breasting the wavelets, observe
The ladies strolling by the tide's hem.

I was part of the décor in this haven,
Made of it a vital ingredient
To teach my students all the better.
I could apply techniques learned
From others who taught with tools
Hewn from hill-palettes of colour,
Impart with a painter's luminosity
Lessons clear as light on water.

THE BIBLE GARDEN IN GLENSTAL

Our herbalist-guide, Fr Brian, explains
The purpose of his plan, its overall design
As we enter this seventeenth century
Terraced garden far from the Lebanon

In Murroe, at the foot of Slieve Felim.
I am reminded of herb shops and musty
Basements, vivid as the stories each plant
Enunciates; their perfumed beds proclaim.

That flowering almond, the last to flower
Before winter's end, signifies fast-moving
Events, our search for answers to ancient
Strife, never-ending struggle for fulfilment

The body and the mind a temple of harmony
Not unlike this lushness where chick-pea,
Dandelion and endive speak to us symbolically,
Urging us not to be enslaved but free.

We glimpse ourselves in each propped mirror
Against the four walls – reminding us
We are part of this growth but like hemlock,
There will be one who conceals a foul odour.

And as the rain begins to fall we incline towards
The lilies of the field, sweet spices and rue
To blossom each side of our homeward path,
Germinate the journey, just and true.

TULLY LANE, FENAGH, COUNTY LEITRIM

for Carmel and Fred

Newly arrived to this once woody place
Near the Mouth of the Great Ford -
McGahern lake country - a poacher's paradise
Concealed by bracelets of shimmering reed
Round Tully Lane - built by locals
For a landlord's congregation
Now silent in its graves.

You hear stories like that from Seamus
In Quinn's pub, folk tales deepening
With every telling in the belly of hills,
Real as Arigna's cramped miners
Drilling all day on their sides,
Headlamps guiding them home
Along the marshy causeways.

There is truth in that because here
You have tapped into locality
With its wing-flap of water-hen,
Clang of teenage drumming.
Freshly rooted, you renew each other
With a welcome that has always
Been yours for the visitor.

...from the margins

How lovely it is today
the sunlight breaks and flickers
on the margin of my book.

Old Irish

FIFTY YEARS OF POETRY

for Knute

Hags Head
is euphoric tonight
as it recites your work
among a timeless
litany deserving
of song.

So listen now
for that Western roar
renewing you
all the way across
the Atlantic
in County Clare.

GOOD HEART
for Chris at sixty

Long life good heart
that beats out time,
fippled and fingered
with unique rhythm.

Such a heart has learned
the tolerance of notes
above the din, rippling
through key holes.

Each breath a precious
second lingering in the ear,
a slide for every minute,
a cut for every year.

HANDS

Behold
two outstretched
headless fish,
finger-fins
hovering
over the earth

Like obedient
soldiers at the ready
for orders to kill
or do some good
for a world
they toil in.

Hard as pick
handles in a coal
miner's shed,
soft and agile
as frolicsome
river-trout

They are seldom
far from water
or drought,
kiss them quick –
before
they disappear.

ON BLINDNESS

For the blind
in a moving car
darkness itself
holds no fear

The danger lies
in what night
brings after
the after-hours

When warped
vision
takes control
of the wheel.

SPINNING TOP

I spied him again
from a stalled
train just when
I had thought
him stopped –
doing his rounds
on the platform,
choosing a spot,
chasing a tail,
dragging life
behind him

Two steps forward,
one step back,
the strain of a saint
in his eyes,
oblivious
to us voyeurs
as we vanished
into the half-moon
above ground,
to spin our own
frenzied lives.

BUNDLES

She knocked gently
Like a child
Sent by a parent
With a stolen toy.

Each time she called
I saw an older woman
with the same glad eye
for what was offered

Knowing only too well
the many possibilities
for an overcoat
given in June.

Each year I heard
a muffled cry
buried beneath
a pramful.

KEEPING FAITH

The ruin stands
with a promise
made to restore
it to its pre-
Cromwellian
glory
by cleaning
out the dung
and shielding
the windy slits
with stained glass.

But stones
vital for salvation
were placed
in modern gables
so that all
within
would be blessed
and protected
by the holiness
of the Abbey's
martyred monks.

EXHIBIT

At first
it was puzzling
to come upon
a nude study
with a halo
over its head.

Everybody
remembered
when they were
innocent,
slept better
than now.

Still,
It was reassuring
to notice a warp
in the halo,
the face wrinkled
by chisel.

SEWING CIRCLES

Those dark days
stirred again
when I read about
the young Afghani poet
Nadia Anjuman,
whose family wanted
her husband to lock
her up because she
frequented literary
gatherings in Herat.
He was a scholar
but that did not stop
him from beating
her to death.

In our society,
within living memory,
people were warned
about the dangers
of close dancing,
evil literature,
cinema-necking.

Vigilante patrols
formed to separate
passionate dancers,
scrutinise book lists,
root out courting couples
with flash lamps.

That was a western
version of moral control
and we may have stopped
short of Taliban rule,
under which a woman
lives her life on a lead,
suffers the consequences
if severed. But we can

Recall being led by wolves
in shepherd's clothing,
who hurt our poets
into song.

THE ORAL TRADITION

My two year old son
drew my attention
with his finger
to a scene
on a street corner
and announced:
Man talking,
talking man.

WHAT'S THE SCENE LIKE HERE?

I have met them
at popular
watering-holes,
hard-up provincials
counting beer money
in the toilets,
befriending
sophisticated
whizz kids
who teach them
how to forget
loneliness.

Some survive
as best they can,
while others
return
to their small-
town origins
talking of red-light
districts
in Amsterdam
and asking
what's the scene
like here?

AFFINITY

Never had he been
So far south.
The furthest he got
Was Ennis.

Because of talk
From young island
Men who bought
Trawler engines

In Cork, he went
To see for him-
Self and found
A curiousity

Equal to his own.
In the pubs
By the Quays
He heard the gulls

And the customers'
Chat rise and fall
Like waves around
His island home.

JOTAELE

Because of an ache
in his bones he set out
with his baggage of love-loss
to probe the boundaries
beyond his tribe.

Immersed in the unknown
he tuned his ear
to its surroundings,
until the dam in his throat
broke, enabling recovery.

Observant of the local
in the frenzy of a volatile
transition, he heard
the widows' sigh
in their fading finery.

Like so many others,
he sought to unlock
the well in his being,
rediscover a language
almost lost to him.

Words like hailstones
melting into his skin,
dissolving along
a swallow-path
in a remote town land

At the base line of silver
birches that clamoured
to reveal some past wrong,
a transient beauty
in the light of it all.

Acknowledgements are due to the following:

Cuadernos de Matemáticas (Madrid, Spain)
Cyphers (Dublin, Ireland)
Natural Bridge (University of Missouri-St. Louis, USA)
The Stony Thursday Book (Limerick, Ireland)
Revival Poetry Journal (Limerick, Ireland)
Tinteán (Melbourne, Australia)
Southword (Cork, Ireland)
Pebble Broadsheet (Limerick, Ireland)